MW01598798

Also by Dean J. Baker

The Herald
The Mythologies Of Love
The Lost Neighborhood
Baker's Bad Boys
Silence Louder Than A Train

Forthcoming: … **Fat Albert's Outpatient Folk Clinic**.. **Soliloquies,** more poetry….

Acknowledgements
Some of the poems here have appeared in:

Descant, Jewish Dialog, Prairie Fire, Northern Light… among others

Front cover photograph ©Cynthia L. Baker

http://deanjbaker.wordpress.com

DARK EARTH

DEAN J. BAKER

INDEX

1 Widows
2 Cleverness
3 A Jealous God
4 Crustaceans
5 Queen St. East
6 October Apples
7 Praying Mantis
8 Masochist And Sadist
9 When We Die
10 Recovery
11 Possession
12 In These Cities
13 Lost And Found
14 I Have Met The Enemy
15 The Boast
16 Bathurst Yards
17 Our Geographies
18 Unspoken
19 See-Saw
20 Insights
21 Considering Our Romance
22 What Wounds Me
23 Modern Prometheus
24 Bread Or Stones
25 Destinations
26 Beauty Stands
27 This Is For You
28 Poetry At Times
29 May Delight
30 Secrets
31 Strawberries
32 Laid Back
33 Precious
34 You Teach Me

35 Antic
36 The Heart At Its Stations
37 I Gave Myself Out
38 The Enigma Of Love
39 The Last Dream
40 Habit
41 Dorian Frog
42 Rejoinder In Denial
43 On The Occasion Of My Divorce
44 Off The Horizons
45 Close Call
46 This Is Poetry
47 Islands
48 Building A Body
49 Alive Again
50 Prophesy
51 All These Poems
52 Fall
53 Dancing
54 Rice Lake, 1962
55 Seduction
56 Chart
57 City Rooms
58 I Don't Know How
59 Fun House
60 The Stupids
61 Pollyanna
62 Allegorical Imperatives
63 Matins
64 Slow Poem For Jane
65 Creatureless Comfort
66 Sex Reared
67 Get Married
68 Invitation
69 Last Romantic
70 The Herald
71 A Friend
72 My Own Idiot
73 Generals Die In Bed
74 A Tourist Observing Ruins

75 Legends Of The Common
76 The Old Lame
77 Coming Of Age
78 The Poetry Hotel
79 The Slow Gathering
80 The Uselessness Of Want
81 This Earth
82 Cassandra
83 Shifting The Ashes
84 L'Enfer
85 Song For Jenny
86 Quod Erat Demonstrandum
87 The Life Of The Sensitive Kid
88 Paper Cancer
89 Dark Earth
90 Initiative
91 Missing Person
92 Fierce Kindness After Breaking
93 Here Is My Pain
94 Beached
95 Over The Shoulder
96 Untitled Habitually
97 Apocalypse Soon
98 You Call Me
99 Just Things
100 Ghost Dancing
101 Horatio Says Not Me
102 Conjugation
103 Blonde Venus
104 Altruistic Ego Dilemma #3
105 Laroe With Grace And Style
106 Mother's Hubbard
107 The Blonde Beauty
108 Audience
109 Where The Heart Resides
110 Invocations, Ulysses
111 Whose
112 In The Dream
113 What You Need
114 Convulsion

115 Haunted Rooms
116 Not That I Am
117 Sharbot Lake
118 Spies
119 Fifth Column
120 Suburban Wilderness
121 On Your Wall

DARK EARTH

DEAN J. BAKER

Widows

Their heads are bent
By another death:
the unlovely child
you always knew too much about.
They are carrying themselves.

They are carrying themselves
With taunts of Spring.
Do you not see how
they drive:
to meet the grinning, opened mouth.

Cleverness

It is you, who have ruined
your life,
with the comparisons

Impatience overworking,
the elegies outworn:
embarrassing

The aborted silence; each
witness unborn: this
poem, and diminuation

A Jealous God

The muse still torments me
every now and then.

I wish her the best; but she
seems almost helpless,
unless the haunting's going on.

She thinks a psychiatrist
may do the trick: forgetting
she had a hand in the mess.

I guess I'm supposed to do
exactly what's expected:
serving as a ghost confessor.

After all, she's lonely
until she finds another life.

Or somebody else to deal with;
who may,
but may not be a stranger.

Crustaceans

Our friends are all dishonest,
because they do not know themselves
for which they cannot be found at fault

Once we might have cursed
their envious gazes, and muttered
rumblings of petty dissatisfaction

Now I thank each one,
for my coveted solitude; and the gift
they never gave materially

Of blessed dignity, and enough
but not too much: knowledge
of their sordid insignificance

Queen St. East

The jaw slacks, with the weight
of the body's loss,
to an inexorable acknowledgement

The brain is unfettered
in its jug; spilling over
with the nostalgia of alcohol

Flat on their backs, near Moss
Park, curled fetus-like, the
inhabitants whirl in a static frenzy of

Enfeeblement, any amusement here
sublingual: the posthumous twitching
of cynics en masse

October Apples

If I walk the long day
out and into evening, perhaps
I shall find that secret place
where we are hiding- no? Well,
you fed me some warm drinks
and conversation; late night talk after
which, could anything that contributed
help but be over-all and genuine?

I thank you for the invitation,
writing from my hotel room. I can
almost see an island waiting – my
requests float back emptily. Nothing
one can say compensates; feelings gone
tell of time and patience: human
again, it is never enough just to maintain.
This happens regularly, love.

Praying Mantis

He dithered and wrote, describing the insects and goats. Worked hard through
railway lands, slobbered through vast expressions of friendship and companionship.
Finally, as a joke decided to feel his way through a girlfriend I once had.

Thus objected, he said he thought it good that if I punched in his loaf and was a better for it to do so.
But only after he'd forgotten to note there'd be no mention of co-writing, no word of co-editing til the child's story was told.

And he entered my own unique title as one of his own. Where he'll linger a tenant, no metal plate in his head from the war: just weary, cheating, an obnoxious ghost.

Talk about bumblebees, insects, and goats.

Masochist and Sadist

Facing each other after years
of self-torment, hatred
or impotent frozen strangulations,
he calls her a whore

She has never been happier, nor
more far from nubial tears;
in her glory at last she
blinds him and two other strangers

With the scalding coffee that
conceals her cold logical crevices;
both are satisfied to be so easily
acquitted: free to begin again

When We Die

When I die, am stiff and cold, old
Bones frozen in the mold; skin grown
Dry and eyes sunk in, opening no more
To witness sun

Where the worms begin to turn
Time backwards, and I don't run:
Lips no more desirous of your kiss, nor
My ears the chime of voices, my mind

The sweet tone of you telling me I am loved
Because my whole body, lying supine
In final clothes, useless and chilled beyond
pavement or stone, which I wish you held now

Warms me once as I have dreamt, a smile
My humor making you laugh, the
Silliness and fun of notes and poems, written
In the luxury of being alive: I know you don't

Think of me thus now, will you then

Recovery

I died in the ambulance,
twice;
both times with you, my
parasite: loving
yet unloved,
in thy vanishing private world,
where the soul
looks out homeward bound

Forgive me if I never loved
you totally; it
was impossible you see;
being imperfect
has certain drawbacks, and
privileges:
the greatest being that the wound
so often smiles back

Possession

I had no language in Athens.
Who could measure for me:
traces of legend, celestial
semen my body made?
Drachmas, shekels, kopeks.

The grief of loss not
mitigated by my bad conscience
crocodiles. The heavy
footsteps of God resound loud:
here's no absent landlord.

What else can he do, but rage,
when the secret is out? Shut
up in this coffin of neurosis,
this is hidden punishment: poor,
to flail about – wonder, gone.

In These Cities

There's eight million, or maybe 4 million, or possibly twelve million souls in the naked city by now, and at least half of them seem to be calling themselves poets.

When I first started writing poems, I think there were eleven, or sixteen. I allowed that there might eventually be a few sub-tribes but that these would be grouped around maybe 20 in total.

I figured this by that fact that the ones who make wonder and light seem to be speaking from inside me, and even now it feels like we're sitting around sharing late afternoon light, a few evenings and some dark nights. They're always present.

We don't even have to be introduced. We know each other. We have nothing to prove, and everything to enjoy. Endless wonder and delight fill our time.

I cherish that time, though it always seems to end.

I have to return to the ordinary world of dead souls, broken dreams, schemes, and mayhem where great engines of the mind lay rusting against many midnights.

Moving through neighborhoods grown wide, work has invaded everywhere. Everyone knows, everyone bows, all are expecting the same, and the sparrows of my youth are nowhere to be seen.

Whenever on my travels I was in the vicinity a poet's house, I'd make a special trip there. I'd go and look up, imagine them and their life, writing and doing. I'd be lost in the immensity of it.

Now I slog through the unrecognizable paths and streets. I pass a hundred roads and avenues, nobody calls my name. The silences have fled, replaced by noise.

Instead there are strangers yelling their names out windows onto the boulevards, certain of cash and fame. Bereft.

I keep walking, making calls which few recognize, eventually sure that one day when I have passed that way, suddenly a porch light will shine in the evening and another timelessness reign.

Lost, and Found

I want to travel over the grade with you again -
go to those clothing shops, stop at the café where
you saw the poster, and we stayed awhile

I miss your company and heat, the rolling hills -
our talks; want to read to you, longer
than we never took to share things literary

The sounds of San Luis resound in my ears -
every day I hear the streets and people, the traffic
the mountains fairly shout at me come back

It is your voice that rings true within everything -
I found and want to discover again, the unimaginable
Tones and chimes you ring and bring me to, believably

I Have Met The Enemy

I have met the enemy,
in my unspoken war:
walking where I went before

Moonlight shatters against the glass:
trolling minor miracles,
like ordinary events no more

There isn't any history tomorrow,
the guests finally departed;
abandoning hysterics, or logic

I wonder whom you will spread
your legs for now, my lovely:
whom you still welcome

Your arms open wide; a
frantic semaphore and deceit
for those desiring rest

Who will come to where I find
no harm, as
they gather there alone inside

Broken swimmers against the tide
of hollow victories:
and these tales of trivial heroics

The Boast

My spirit lover, my finger
is damp with the self-respect
which some call angel dust.

It falls softly as snow
from the dehydrated organs,
pinned fiercely against this wall.

Standing up where I once stood,
to confront us in our lies:
rarely admitted before proven, my enemy.

Follow that direction if you can.
There's no way out or divorce, from this
 ill-fitting span of time, darling.

You don't have to put anything on.

Bathurst Yards

Sprawled in this boxcar apartment,
no one's serious
the disturbance temporary

The end of the line,
the lock breaks -
the cargo falls out over-ripe

We shall never get there;
blueprints and maps
do not provide an idea of progress

Which does not matter,
stepping from the rails
to meet familiar ground

Watching how the sun I own
goes down through these trees:
our wings, folded like those leaves

Our Geographies

Whatever you felt for me,
could not
be measured by any shift of luck;
nor movement in the earth's
degrees,
treasured by sight and sound:
varied
within the small voids of the unexpected

Breeze, that blows around
and down
beside the hills; and valley
contours
contained throughout: our final assent
beyond latitudes, or
the wisdom of unsuspected, unknown attitudes

Unspoken

Give me an excuse
for another
poem or song

Made to order, especially
the times you cannot sing or speak,
that make a certain melody

Only you and I shall
ever understand:
as we do now silently

See-Saw

The soft susurrus
of snow
blows over my dreams,
of you and I
in deep warmth -
sweating, from our fucking
or intercourse: sweet

Conversation
I had not known,
missing,
before you breathed truth into me

Insights

I have no time for pity
who would make time for loving you;
the city contrives
the boredom, and continued heartbreaks
that would stop
any but the gods' favored
sons and daughters: distilling from
their undiluted rage and pain
a sorrowful knowledge, which

Takes the shape of perfect
pearls of wisdom the infected delude
themselves are manifest for their vision;
when they're blind even to the sun
beneath which I dance and run,
playing for a silent audience, whose
applause is as the sound of one:
who gives meaning to
both darkness and the heavens above

Considering Our Romance

You're not with me these nights,
in which the silence
pounds inextricably
down the throughways of my blood

I could tell your presence
immediately; by the shining, altered
radiance of certain
stars singling us out for their light

But that was an illusion,
as the star
fades back into night –
impossible to capture with the mind alone

The reasons quite explanatory,
suffer themselves to endure
the worth of all things:
whatever distant name I bring is yours

What Wounds Me

What wounds me is everything;
the dead streets, the blinded flesh.
Your indifference and sad enthusiasm.
Hotel rooms without women.
No work done, no food.

A strange ability I have. Pain
not to be endured
becomes necessary infliction.
It does not sustain me:
I have starved myself to bone.

Shattered when the unnatural feast
is reasonably made stone,
I meet this slaughter everywhere.

Modern Prometheus

I've been stranded in this blizzard
for what seems like eons.
I can't tell exactly when I froze.
If you happen to be in the mood,
you may notice I am transparent.

I just had to tell someone.
During an experiment, or adventure,
you will meet the shield of snow.

Think of it as your parents, a passport,
The government: anything a vacation
could cure. I assure you it is none.

We are not travelling towards death,
who laughs at our metaphysical impotence;
We are gesturing for the storm to stop.
It's no sheet of ice whereon we play:
this mercy, in the upturned palm of God.

Bread Or Stones

We were just fucking, there
isn't any commitment
to speak of; insults and
humiliations pass
in a hurt grace that halts
any attempt
at growth, or uncovering:
the fear to which we sacrifice
daily our love

Prometheus could not be
more pleased
with our maneuvering deceit;
or the delight
we take in such cannibalism
with the promised feast,
always and forever,
beyond the reach of these:
fools, who never stop touching themselves

Destinations

Our headaches: what about
my several hours of sickness

The opium
of ceaseless food –

Nobody caring, and you
refusing to serve a term

For one room in this hotel
on the moon

All that was unborn
takes its place beside you, now

Beauty Stands

Beauty stands in sparrow clothes,
Almost abandoned, sure her love
Life will prove satisfactory this time;
Growth unimpeded, she knows
Knowledge is the greater choice, though
She cannot get beyond her own

Appearance and charm, at least
What I think does not prove harmful;
Allowing hope to stretch between us
Unspoken, unwished for, called
Into being that embraces her finally in warmth:
Where she is no longer her own vain ghost

This Is For You

This is for the girl for whom I'm a new obsession. This is for the
fools who never learn their lessons.
This is for you who believe you see what I write, in disappearing
ink, in the middle of the long night.

This is for the song thief who believes so long he thinks it's his
own.

This is for the crowd of those who wander around under the moon
assaulting killer clowns. This is for those who betray with a
whisper, who feed on glass, and expect satin slippers.

This is for you who think highly. This is for you who smile slyly.
This is for those who refuse, for those who think it's a joke.

This is for the low and mighty, the high and corrupt. This is for all
those not exempt.

This is for the girl with a kitten, the boy with a mitten; the old coot
with a dog, the old woman without clogs.

This is for knowing what you always have known. This is for
getting over and beyond.

This is for the liars and betrayers who speak with one voice and
give strength to the slayers.

This is for me, the artist and writer, the musician and friend, the
son and lover.

This is your time, there is no other. This is for giving whatever you
get.

This is a song, not a poem or a prayer.

This is for those who don't know the difference.

Poetry At Times

Poetry does not matter, you aren't
Beside me; and we don't speak

What are words without you, but
Whispers in the dark to keep

The ghosts away who gather round
The only ones who celebrate

This ache and mystery, as long as
They can resume center stage again

May Delight

What can be said regarding your beauty
you have not heard expressed tirelessly
before? Your smile and lips – the soft
swell of your breasts, rising
the rhythm of your curving, slender hips?
No way to know the woman and the girl.

In those pictures the goddess holds sway -
The slight upturn of your smile, the hint
of playfulness – these are all
which betray the sudden delight, within
the radius of your company: that gift
you freely bring simply by being alive today.

Secrets

The depth of my soul cannot be measured by the lack of currency
in my possession.
The coins of your success do not notch failure in my heart, which
lies forever in your thoughts.
Many talented Golem walk, wander the streets of cities, such as
Nashville and Toronto, convinced of their importance. They light
the pages of the military's internet.
They are not my army. But your conscripts into the columns,
churning
towards honey and God amid the eternal dust.

The secret you keep from everyone is: nothing you have or possess
will be kept safe; everything will be taken, everyone lost is already
found,
nothing you task is sacred or profound.

I am the thief who has stolen these moments, remaining
unconvinced the poet's garret suggests anything, but the poverty of
your own inabilities you please yourselves to call imaginations.

More wealth is mine than you could dream. And that is how I keep
the world of your possessions, with a benediction and a song: a
heartbeat.

Dance now, in your cage of bones, as the flames burn higher.
Don't
ask me to help when all along I have done what I can, offered
sustenance:
thrown all things up in the air the better to be seen.

And all you've done is to dispatch the crows to steal the shining
stars
and pretty things you could never hope to own.

This is the embrace, the kiss you have been waiting for: a secret even
now you have lusted after, and towards.

There is no end.

Strawberries

Today I bought strawberries -
luscious, red and ripe, bright with
sunshine and juicy inside

I promise when I bite into them
my only thoughts will be:
of you undressed and waiting for me

Laid Back

Take your petty arguments,
The vehicles of contrition;
By which you damn and bless,
Those unlucky enough
To be near you in this mess

And poison yourselves; die
To the world, my children,
Before you ever dare assume
Your life has any more significance
Than the doom or hell you spread

Sowing barren misery and defeat,
The disease rotting out
Your lungs, liver, and kidneys:
Fear as well as hate will stop, when
The cancer in you is dead and gone

Precious

My little feral cat sits straight-backed, at
attention, facing the backyard wilderness -
reminiscing at the bargain she's made

Black and white, non descript, ordinary,
she might pass you by unremarked, a
world of tender and foul curiosities, yet

A fine judge of character, more aware
than you or I in any circumstance, this creature
in whose ignorance we mighty triumph

Fodder for the wheels of giants, the
mechanics of sentiment and denial, she
is now your only chance to avoid your philosophy

You Teach Me

I thought I was familiar
With the lost art of conversation

When I had
Forgotten in your presence

Desire speaks,
Another language I must unlearn

As love enters in,
A stranger arrogant and unwilling

Antic

Goddamn the penny
Ante satanic antics of everyday

Adversarial lies that pass
As discussion, in which you

Assume, graceless
You're above the fray

Competition you made
For a self

A mere ego stroke away
From having its heart

Attack itself in protest of the narcissism
And die

Suddenly disabused
Of the notion that others do not remain

Puppets in your museum
That monument to unholy lies

You enshrine until
The idea of sacrifice is suicide

The unpetalling of a rose
Your only crime

The Heart At Its Stations

Love has captured you for us,
my darling; love has taken hold:
you are no more enamored
of girlfriends and the anonymous
boring goal of telling stories,
that belong to no one else of your fold

Love has you in its raptures,
my dearest; and hopes you'll be bold
to escape the fear of self-hatred,
so many before me told: that
you know your solitary state is
only enriched by this other soul

Love sets you in the deluge,
where all has come to pass; and you
believe with eyes wide open
now everything will last: but choose,
the focus of your speech as each wind
moves almost silently, through the stricken grasses

I Gave Myself Out

I gave myself out so nakedly
You turned back
The scent
The door
The key

I was left standing blatantly
A lack, alas
Spent
Bereft
On my knees

The Enigma Of Love

I love you and I always will.
You're beautiful.
Is that what you want? For
me to be telling lies, or

Have I, as usual,
misunderstood; and erring,
not chosen,
those niceties you most cherish

The Last Dream

Your wrists wrapped in hospital gauze;
You tugging at receding shirt sleeves,
to conceal the self-inflicted
wounds, I entered your life
in the café where we were stranded:
alone in our separate ways,
neither wondering about anyone else

Sitting beside me, your eyes
unable to conceal a hatred of loneliness;
that I would be more than you'd divine
with your careless intelligence, that
we would stop the hothouse loss of
unusual growth: the last dream
cradled in obscene slashes of cold reality

Habit

Ashes in my mouth –
the tongue's
an old dog blanket:
for one who's gone south

But I can't see yet –
my eyes burn,
and grind:
little particles falling out
chart a general decay

It doesn't mean anywhere else,
which my gutrot attests;
when the headbone is: not another
hollow loaf of stale regrets

I refuse to change –
I am the best I know, so
what if I'm going blind:
time is an enemy,
held like a stone in my heart

Dorian Frog

The man who scribbles verse, toad-like
about insects and worse, has perfectly
described his mean lack of character

He is a shadow of all his work;
no portion exempt from self-contempt:
to disguise a transformation he needn't go after

The vampires staked; the drunks hauled into the shade,
the unlovely virgins unmade:
his excremental vision has flushed the fraud away

A Rejoinder In Denial

Next time you try to shit on me, love,
set me on fire too; so I can
know what it's like:
to truly burn, and finally

Neither be confused, nor mistaken
as to the origin
of both the smell and the smoke:
when you feel threatened and alone

On The Occasion Of My Divorce

I had to become
better acquainted with myself

Knowing you, I
didn't want to know anyone else

Off The Horizons

We made our way along the Perfume River, far
Past the Bridge of Sighs, no longer near
The Golden Mile we slide across
Bayou de Chien, arising into Tennessean hills,
Desirous of good company, wild sex, and food -
Maybe a gun or two to keep away the jackals

Stepping onto pavement, moving through rooms
Anchored by a wondrous joy and solitude,
No longer bound by false beliefs
Of the frozen multitudes demanding restitution,
We are free of idiots: leaning into the Caribbean
Breeze, bringing nothing with which we cannot deal

Close Call

I'm such a stumbling, mumbling clown,
where the sure, deft touch of gentleness
requires an artist; that you be not bereft,
exposed to the elements, which
place you there as though a guest
at the happenstance of your own life: frozen

Through cruel jokes made or played, unless
you come in from the cold that has plagued
all you've known; and admit nothing less
than the bitterness and rage:
flung out to gather me into your arms again,
as we advance beyond the trackless sand and snow

This Is Poetry

This is poetry
I'm sorry I don't
agonize over the poem
I apologize for everything
spoken, and unknown
I repent my deeds
Misinterpreted, or not
my torment won't be forced
I acknowledge
you are the final arbiters of taste
I do admit
I investigate emotion
with my thousand bad habits
yet I still own the lines
and music, you would supervise
though you will allow
others to tell you otherwise
I know if I succeed
I have earned your praise and lust
If I have displeased
I must be shown
the multiple errors of my way
but I confess to nothing
In this experiment
of sunsets and slaughter
where you always know
more than I could hope to show
I am the music
I am the poem

Islands

I've been stumbling a lot recently;
though our late night walks,
well worth the pace,
mean more than any comment I make.

Autumn leaves in their rotting
browns and reds betray us. We
cannot compete with such litter
of the season: sweet desolation.

Even if one were so lost as the wind,
over this wide world, I know
you beneath the stars and how
I moved away: delighting in your company.

Building A Body

I'm building a body, broken
And scarred; patched with lesions, raw
Red welts that pinch and pain, surface
A coal-bedded fire I can't do without

And I'm surfacing with it, amongst
Duty and details, neglectful friends
and a brother casting doubt on everything
of whatever is not gold and cold

I'm taking this disintegration seriously
I am hauling the carcass on top
Of a hill, where this torn Prometheus
Can shout, or whisper, this is what you wanted

Are you happy now, do you congratulate
Yourselves on your select sensitivity
Do you not know you will be
Judging yourself exactly as you have left me

Alive Again

I'd drive the Cabot Trail, the twists
around ocean and peak; spread greens
beyond boundaries of water or land, arising
then through Algonquin's forested, yet pale
highway pulling me through – admire endlessly
the western ocean as I sail beside islands, slipping
down the Pacific Coast, a ghost then
of who I am and have become: mired in majesty

Running through Camden Town, or
dodging traffic along the Via Veneto, while
standing amidst the fields of Donegal as I arrive
past the startled tourists that litter my history -
in front of the lake, behind the trees, on
the steppes of progress inhabiting the sheer beauty
of being alive in this land I own again, grateful
I sense grace however momentarily its swift refrain

Prophesy

I scribble here to what effect -
we honor ourselves too much, I expect

I never know what comes next:
the grass grows, the wind blows

And the weather truly sucks at best

All These Poems

All the poems, the notes, old
melodies silent for now;
every single line and inspiration,
muddled or divine, remain simply
words known and rearranged

Vowels conjugated and held
softly and often in my throat, my love;
each one a wonder and surprise,
each my call to you:
my song, my hallelujah of your name

Fall

I love the odor of decaying leaves;
The smell of death, the scent of grief:
In every hue and color
A widow's wrist, thin and brief

The absence that I feel in everything
Dear friends gone, amid
The fog through the streets
The nip of a winter winding-sheet

The spirit of our live asleep
The aspect of each object incomplete
Without recurring seasons, none
Escape nor dare not celebrate this evening

Dancing

Let's lie beneath the sheets
these days and nights; where
I surround you impossibly,
touching me at my leisure

Our purity not too strong
nor sickly romantic,
ever for boredom or distaste:
as we perform desire and disgrace

And finally, in your arms
let's go dancing,
beneath the mirrored
shining lights of city and sky

We dance the years, we
dance away our fears;
we are alone:
in this body too often our delight

Rice Lake, 1962

Why
did no one tell me
about the poet-kings
and the slow collision of light

That summer went by,
like an unlocated sound
of night,
spent on other shores

I was too young
for fire or the gasoline banquet;
burned instead
in your different breath

The wound open
to visitors and praise;
like the list of names, only
secret to ourselves

Seduction

You've been on
my mind, awhile

Slide
down

a little further
and

we can both get comfortable

Chart

I want to live alone -
Our words
Reaching only each other;
Where no man comes to shout
His name in my face
Until I have found yours:
Which I use to blacken these pages
And from the shifting pieces

Ornament my walls,
As though prints of the Japanese artists
Came cheaply;
As memories I had erected,
And forgotten either reason or motive
For their eventual destruction and betrayal:
As if love could keep terror out,
Or all our secrets in

City Rooms

He says
Sing a song of
what city
and what lost girl

I didn't want to go down
I saw you on the edge;
threads tossed like ribbons
tied inside your teeth

One face and the pavement,
grey in November dawn;
smoky as an all-night restaurant,
clean as the wanderer moon:

There's nowhere I could go

I Don't Know How

I don't know how to escape
the cage of slums,
in which I live; wanted
by none, desired by many

For my ills, there's no sum
equal to the cure;
nor any analgesic to mitigate
the spasms of joy

You can see how my face
is contorted with one now: your
silence more mysterious to me,
than what I have to say of love

Fun House

Like everything
that went uncompleted – the people,
poems and books, anonymous:
old inspiration contained

It could be met
among hated prospects of the world;
until nothing would do,
but midnight and certain constellations

I undress your body,
when you are not talking; quiet
while I step away:
the swarm of mirrors a cold embrace

The Stupids

My mind's a thread unwinding; I
pluck at darkness, which falls.
It won't let the stupids out; it
suffers them to bray and shout,
these Attic businessmen and women:
busy, they are knitting spirit doilies.

Must I endure like a disease the bad
and bright side of the living's enemies?
But who am I asking? We are so
few than farther between might be.

You cannot hear me; you are denying everything,
soiled by the crossways unclean:
strapped in a cocoon of the secondary.

Pollyanna

I'm not going to kill
myself;
for you, or any other cunt:
I am free and beautiful

You can do what you want,
or thought you could;
when I was your slave,
and you were the maiden who would

Allegorical Imperatives

The wounded bears of this belated land,
trailing deceit; and a lingering death:
bore me with their appraisals of excellence.

Accomplices to culture still-born, these
picayune mediocrities forge no sense
of self: damage or display, apologists.

You do well to beware such politics;
domestic confederates, nationalist failures:
the talented and their imitators.

Let them vanish into the forest deep, where
I have set up a meditation and a prayer:
forecasting sudden but true, and rare transformation.

Matins

When you are soaked with love,
the dream come true, flesh
meeting flesh, which those two minds
direct; neither from below nor above,
I fold up in you, renewing stealth.

Only as it should be, needing
no comment from us, who speak
in syllables of silence and deceit:
the past a death we live through,
hand-in-hand with each stalled move.

I take your sigh, place the wish
upon my neck; the embrace
sets free both night and day, we
hold the light against dead time: suddenly,
call the miracle to task again.

Slow Poem For Jane

I don't know if I want
to kill you
like the million other
killers the city gives refuge to.

I take on the shape of what is close.
I am nothing in particular.
To some I am a ghost.
This is all my love:
These lines, this page, the troubled notes.

I don't ask you
when you're leaving.
I let you know I am alive and well.

Creatureless Comfort

I watch the skin of my brother's leg
peel back, set to flame;
uncurling
cardboard, turning slowly black.

I cannot change, remain the
same for ages;
able to do anything, yet
unwilling in the final stages.

I find blame in the least thing.
I implicate, sentence;
execute:
it doesn't matter what you say.

Sex Reared

Sex reared its ugly head
She said -
So I took her to bed

She didn't have to
Worry or wonder, or
Be smart instead

Sexed her rear,
Vexed her tears:
Oh, what an ass I led

Get Married

You go into the city from your provincial fleapit, expecting
friends and meditation.
A friend, who happens to be female, at this or any other time
does and does not object to kisses.

But she has been attacked in one day by a 12 yr old pervert, a
moaning female dwarf named Myra; and a cretinous slob who
works
the city's transit system in search of virginal passengers.

You come back from the maze, your friend is Circe – any other
pal lies and delays.
The countryside is a cesspool the city abrogates, bullies
into the idyllic.

A lover has turned sour, regimenting housework; and under
all their insect gaze, you are just as small.

Invitation

You've caught me with
my suicide mask wearing thin -
Death, an old sidekick
and various forms of unrequited love;
accompanied by
virgin humiliation,
strike the bone of the ghost-ridden
music that echoes in the
hollow of my heart

I want you to take
some of your old medicine;
this hate, this emaciated bitterness
and the dehydration of the body,
the loveless trough
throat and lungs make amid the unheard

Pulsing of a sick sun
in the pumped-out stomach ache.
God, I'm tired of being late -
suiting my person to a fool's
tailor who labors blind for the emperor;
and does not know
the difference between desire and dust:
nor these odd goodbye scenes
conveying no taste of
the final, approaching lust

Last Romantic

Your skin is:
a cool whisper
on my hot flesh, and

In the delicate, yet
perfect island
of your ear, I'd swear

I, who am blind, could
hear and see:
the one miracle of eternity

The Herald

Nothing more than abstract ornament,
explanations and discussions
keeping us to ourselves; we were
too petty for anything else. God
and Spirit, man and God again: no
insight into the common denominators.

Stupidity categorized the crews
taking over. In Canada, one was
reduced to waiting; at best,
you sent yourself notes (not poems)
hoping they would stay closed, or
fall open revealing all upon arrival.

You are lost either way. Death
enters your life: a troubadour
strolling through the provincial town.
Each gesture of government singing
the unwanted guest to bed, who is
finishing the last bite of food.

One brought no plans for conversation,
issuing invitations in the dark
he slips from his clothes. The livery
stark amusement, leaving only the arc
of a streetlamp which constellates:
the hard vistas of distant expectation.

A Friend
for John Newlove

You don't like marriage,
but you like the company.

We've bent our elbows
so long on the same drink:
one of us must be a mirage.

Do you think that this
is how it ends – a little
blood spilled, sinking?

That's not the moon; white
and propitiated,
sweeping cobwebs off your shoulder.

You tell me to listen:
as if belief may do more
than conjure truth.

My Own Idiot

You, my dear anorexic,
the lost child;
on whom darkness shuts,
become invisible

But who was always missing;
golden boy, or girl:
the world a strange hissing,
dumb fears

With which you cannot fly,
from the terror;
the rage threatening:
thy holy resolution to be perfect

Yet nobody divines the truth,
and you imagine
that finally it has come to this:
when you know it's not been different

An ultimate conspiracy; at last
you strangle forever:
knowing there are no villains,
and the goal is to never arrive

"Generals Die In Bed"

no time for diffidence; the dream
of death, ordinary:
and inconvenient, leaving debts
we should have left anyway

those ghosts bleed into history,
thickening everything; the next
step may lead anywhere:
choose carefully with whom you associate

in admiration of the WW1 book **Generals Die In Bed** *by Charles
Yale Harrison*

A Tourist Observing Ruins

This house is so broken,
with the images
of what might have been;
the last experiment
a scientist's shattered facilities,
a chemical residue

There is no cure for what
you think of tomorrow:
the hero in northern absences,
abandoned on an R.C.M.P post; perhaps
dying of tuberculosis in Rome,
longing to say 'I did return'

While you and I are two guests
in the burned-out town,
survivors open to investigation;
departing into no sudden sunsets,
amid this most ordinary life:
of quarrels, and lovers gone

Legends of the Common

Something attracts. I assume we're powerless to guess.
We seem innocent. It may be lack of imagination; what the
ordinary world supports.
That vitiation.

Those who sing are well aware that traveling is our
destination. You think you have a guarantee; but old fears
creep… and I am drunk on your lawn before the sun comes up.

You allow this, being generous with moral applause. The
sleepless will.
So superstitious that you believe anything before you
are told.

The Old Lame

I turn my head.
It's useless to talk about lacking external experiences.
The intense nerve slides forward apace with such taunting; the
last point of departure you're trained to: the main chance.

Various fictions a deliberate version of age without sexuality.
For the young and old at genital? Or merely toward each other as
good policy?
Whose nightmare?

I tire of those fools. You too, I see. It is better than the dancing
bear's skill
to rest among sleepers crowded into one room like a fever.

The velvet nights, narrow; the white, excised.

Coming Of Age

I guess I knew it would have me
before I could consent to happiness.
To admit that I dream a different
being every night: awake,
within another life fools only contemplate.

I am speaking to you from the future.
Far ahead of myself I can't explain
why I enjoy the company of women more
so than the battalion of boys: I
don't like the unfeminine obscenities.

Dallying with self – hate it doesn't sing –
I bleed, I show everything.
I am not the breed to complain; no
longer content with the divorce between
the suggestion of excellence and success.

I have come of age amid clichés; this
pain the price I pay and pay. You
can proceed unharmed, but changed: dust
anyway, you dance clutching at decay.
My lepers so brave, you go away. Away.

The Poetry Hotel

Throw yourself from these heights imagining some may care.
A last act of charity taking the world in tow.
Think of those waiting in the vaults of this city.

Reason sweetly until you climb the tower. Swing from a cozened
bent of normality.
Step from your corner.

Parents are the first to go. Vermin sucking at your child's heel
next.
You forgive your dreams gradually. Once, you preferred roses.

Who's left? Statistics don't count.

But nothing was supposed to smell like this, you stupid ghost.

The Slow Gathering

Down on your knees,
you are the Word:
made flesh

We shall allow to develop,
into this:
suddenly more real

Creating
a world,
we move toward by slow degrees

The Uselessness Of Want

You seem eager
to be gone, my dear
mother; shrunk
upon the pillow, your

anemic swirl of hair
twists to a dying curl,
curiously mouthing
the inarticulate word

the sentence done:
as if you were an acquaintance
hurt into further distance,
your soul pointedly surprised.

This Earth

What was I running from
when everything was
beside me

Shaking at the thought
of you, inside
each move I made

When I couldn't say
who was called that night
into silence

whispering
in my pain
You

You
 it is myself
I come upon like this

Cassandra

This poem has kept me up
two nights

Not that you're responsible -
I've been waiting too long

And though it's late,
the lights are on.

But now it's dark
as dark between the sleepers

Who gather beneath this toadstool,
Midget lawyers of professional corner advice

In a room I never use:
we can't seem to be quiet about you, child.

What could I do
about official feasts -

Could I provide my grandfather's excuse
and his high collar like this

The way wild, sly women
take their place

Beside a man
too weary for waiting.

Now the world
appears among your guests

Suddenly apparent and unwelcome
as an anonymous donor

The company stands around:
you are sick into the night.

Shifting The Ashes

I turn on the switch,
for the kitchen light:
nothing stirs.
Your shadow at first
dark as space,
fades and falls behind.

The streets climb into silence,
listening for
the pulse of evening in your step.
Where you come clean:
as bare-ribbed winter trees

Thrust against the threatening sky.

L'Enfer

It must be like
this: not knowing
where the conversation collapsed
when there is no one left
to talk to

And silence
breaks in upon you
as though a sudden guest
had coughed politely for attention
in some corner of the house

Song For Jenny

Mad-
ness hums in my ear,
like a fly
that's caught there.

I can't touch you.
This is
the new ballet.
I can't touch you.

Stay away,
I am deaf with silences.
Splintered and shining,
I go down like a stone.

Quod Erat Demonstrandum

By their actions, not by their words -
By the behavior, not the sentiment
Of sheathed swords; by the buried
Feelings unseen and unheard, unless
You hear between the syllables
And silence, the language of the unspoken

By what's known and unknown, not
What's agreed upon and conferred;
By a certain willingness to not be first,
By what's disclosed, not the requested joke:
Of the one thing you should know
Before you pass into the realms of fog

By what is not required to admit access,
By what is told to you alone, not mocked
By a million friends who are all special too;
By the trust held close, the vow not lost:
Freedom to be wrong without harm, by these
Things unsaid and not chosen as we go

The Life Of The Sensitive Kid

Pretending poverty, I am rude with feeling.

I slap babies. I have drunk the moon at high tide.
And these papers will be worth some dollars, some day.

I sit, sloop-shouldered in bars of the nation.

I ask for nothing, I know my part.
I don't pray revenge.

It may all happen.

Paper Cancer

I'm dying of a paper cancer; folded
smaller by the night, the
envelope of sky no address
you can find me by in the cold
stars that burn –
the old way no one's ever been:
and lived to tell except through change
the ceaseless unforgiving motion rearranges

But damn this contrary maze, that
does not allow recognition
of paralysis due to denial and desire;
dampening then fuelling every fire
toward the one I most hunger for – sabotage
requires no other device than this
sin of omission: dividing myself,
from the knowledge to which I aspire

Dark Earth

Two weeks without you; not in
nor anywhere but about, is a long
lie: which may contain the truth,
or let it out again.

I have kept on waiting, simply
impatient; relishing the pain of
separation:
though like two twigs we wind
into one another, bind the common root.

Initiative

I'd ravish that young blonde
at the table nearby, without a qualm

If I could escape their indulgent attitude;
and punishment, for having revealed

The indiscretion, or cruelty
they can now only harbor second-hand

Missing Person

Every time I look
into your eyes,
there's another man
disappearing for cigarettes
out the front door

And down the block

Don't you think it's
about time,
you let me in
past the glass eye since
you know finally

Who it is really knocking

Here Is My Pain
"Wachet Auf" – Bach, Cantata 140

Here is my pain-
this is my blood;
just pinch a vein:
it flows down upon the page

Though this may seem complete –
poem and song as food;
taste the dying mood: know
you are bone, and mud

God forgive my enemies –
love forget my friends;
let art come to each:
in the form of their belief

Where my bed is made,
old sheets are stripped clean;
the marriage is dissolved:
the children come back again

Beached

I need to run my tongue
Over the thigh, and ass
Of that woman alight in the sand

Smiling as I take in the hair
And her eyes
The smile that brings everything

Maybe even say I'm interested
As long as I get to glance
At those photographs in my mind

Over The Shoulder

I have stared hungrily,
into the eyes
of a hundred, anonymous
women: and
found as many, staring back

I suppose the problem,
if we must call it
something new; could be solved,
should she and I manage to
discuss this in our mutual solitudes

Untitled Habitually

The girl I desire is sadder
than the gray day;
tossing its threadbare
ribbons
like scattered crows

Alighting
on memory's shoulder,
in a hurricane of loss:
more change she cannot forget,
until she dares to remember this

You Call Me

You call me up from the dead, begging
support and sympathy you know you'll get

Far from the Arctic chill you've let surround
the frozen chaos of your heart, addicted

To being everyone's fulfillment of need, you're
spent before you can take a next breath,

With no end but charity you do not give
yourself or me, who does not exist

For you in any warm regret, except as
a debt where you extract interest again, and again

Until neither you nor I can do anything about this:
since there are no more fences to jump, or mend

Apocalypse, Soon

If I've been walking on air
these past weeks, then
I would doubt the too solid ground
as being simply ephemeral

It's the same with questions,
answers I give;
I can do nothing, unless
you believe in more than reason

My knees are raw
from our love-making, haven't
you heard of elbows blossoming:
such stigmata holy evidence

Just Things

Things are different now
as you know:
they change with words, altering all

That's ok I say, don't mind
 me, or you:
changing always with what you altar too

Ghost Dancing

The burden you will always carry
has metamorphosed into your son, father.
And just as your father did to you
so you have tried with me, but failed.
I learned to hate lies an untruth:
before you ever had a chance to succeed.
I know that you have always had to protect
yourself; from the awareness of beauty shared:
you were taught by practical matters
the world could be seen
through a grid or matrix of black and white.
Wrong and right still dominate there,
where success is the highest pinnacle; but
who can hide from the long reach of death?

You live with the phantoms of an unrehearsed
youth; and I carry the corpse of my childhood
with me: the prison bars do not serve,
except to obscure our separate realities.
In this moment we are more similar than
different; comically we believe we hate
each other, at least you feel this about me.
I often wish I could be as unrelievedly
ignorant; without wonder too, absolutely certain.
You dismiss me as a cretin, an idiot at times, yet
who isn't? And I confess I share that state of grace:
with you in your lovelessness, when you
abandon me to a fate you have never escaped.

Your mother is dead, as is mine; and my wife
Has succumbed to another kind of cancer, but
One that is just as deadly: you don't
Know, until afterwards whenever it's too late.
Between you and I, the battle rages; because
I cannot live your life,
While you resent the advantages of mine:
The comparison does not hold and we grow old.
You will never understand that I love you, a cliché,
the only way I know; and refuse to accept
that such care must take the form of punishment,
the denial of a life you do not own.
You are alone and a cancer has you by the throat -
there are no more stones left to throw: we
strangers are shadows now, ghosts dancing on the wall.

Horatio Says Not Me

I'm not falling, that's too silly
I'm not writing poems for you
I'm not staring at your picture

Imagining how you move, hearing
Your voice
What your scent must be like

How you shine differently
Morning, and southern nights
No, not me

I did not write this, either by the way

Conjugation

This is the way we make love -
Words back and forth, innocent
Repartee and almost hidden
From ourselves, but she knows
I wouldn't quit; she's ideal, and

Though we might never meet
She could say yes any day; I'd be
More than ready every way, my
Vowels in place for greater conjugation:
Literature, my aim and obligation

Blonde Venus

You don't have to be blonde for me. Or sit lonely in coffeehouses past midnight until your room in the ancestral home on Bedford Ave. is emptied of its ghosts for the final time.

*

Everyone grown flabby behind the carnival light.
We won't stop assuming commerce: disguising the scream.

The teeth rust, the gut slumps. A perfect fire.

*

Where can you go to get warm before the burning's done?
Return to the cawled shadows.

*

It's always the first bruise gloriously won.

Altruistic Ego Dilemma #3
For Cindy

Tell me a story of love fulfilled; the
feudal lord and peasants, friends;
over the distant fields, where animals
run from the patchwork land:

into other territory they do not comprehend,
leads to their slaughter and final destiny

They do not have to travel to find glory,
nor seek refuge in their different stories;
there a rainbow bends from the base
of the skull to the foreign eye: we,

my love, should learn such lessons,
as they teach who roam within the mind

Laroe, With Grace and Style

I know I should be happy
My best friend never keeps his word
Nor apologizes, merely announces
His troubles are the reason
Then I met a woman I could like,
And he tells me she's the apple of his eye

Another grateful lady is polite, and
Kind; hating to be bored or idle, so
She has only time for her work, not me –
Whom she studies from the bar
Distance being the safest course, my Laroe
Can imagine
For what she's willing to know

I'm so happy I'm almost delirious
I recommend you try this
At the next possible moment; you
Don't have to be shy, though, or wonder
If, after all, there is another road:
This is the destination always desired
The vision a truth she has embraced, and inspired

Mother's Hubbard

Why should I in my freedom
my sunlight
be the one to save you,
from your hopelessly conventional
wisdom and fear?
I refuse to serve, to sacrifice:
the national alibi.

Really, you can go fuck yourself.
I'm busy in the corner
with Susie Horner,
and we're cutting ourselves a share
of the pie: our throats pipe the music.
You couldn't be my good luck charm,
nor hold a tatter to the wind if you tried.

The Blonde Beauty

You may consider my passion quite tenuous: that's another marvel of this collective age.

And she was no goose. Why else did I see her? I am no philosophe.

*

I held my own dead seriousness at that tombstone stop. Time of the next bus, bookworm… why, yes. Aske me ye anythinge.
Hell, I couldn't speak nor grasp the idea.

We were suspended in mutual tension.

*

I imagine the pressure of appreciation.
The obsequious arrogance; of wee, well-meant answers as gestures.

Mystery no trick, it's a disguise to take advantage of one's own wealth undisturbed.

*

No one bothered to look.

*

Though I could have watched forever, and probably do.

Audience

What I write I want to slip
into your synapses, light the fuse
against nerve endings that
the mind already knows, without

Instruction or tools; to right the
balance of the world, and recognize
what cannot yet be done but proceeds
as your flesh tingles, the flush sweeps

Tiny hairs against the dreaming thighs, which

Wash clean all thoughts of what is
right and wrong, acknowledging only
feelings that bring you to yourself, again;
forgetfully until you need to stretch

Your legs and limbs, rushing streams
against the horizon of skin and the aching
dawn between your legs flowing faster
than you can stop the secret welcome: that

Delicious flood of memories to be made

Where The Heart Resides

Wind rolls across the window, waves
of rain thrown against the pane; on Morro St.
the night's so impenetrable, yet I imagine
stars wheel over Higuera, while the mountains
remain there for your morning view -
here everything's almost unfathomable and gray

I'm not even visiting, displaced events take
precedence over the truth, so
you're safe it seems for the moment,
at the other end of this communication; I
hand paper over, electronic transmittal:
our hands meeting in inner space, only a leap

Can make the past and present meet, brave
forever in the face of things and people saying -
Yes, we play for keeps, we dance
amid the stars and streets, soloists together:
unpopulated by even the bright memories,
we admit you and I have yet to make, and will again

Invocations, Ulysses

1

Love here, I think, does not mean
very much. It's rather boring, shoddy
and stained; a greasy adventure
in political kitchens. You're a fool
to imagine it would.

2

Not diving to the heart,
not daring to be seen or heard; but
faulting on the peripheries, sweeping chaos:
this middle-class geography of passion
keeps us.

3

Year after continuous year, seasons
beneath the gray ocean tide
swelling at once and often with pain;
the telling debris, the imminent disaster:
the proud foam of fabled humanity.

Whose

I wish you would come over
I wish you would
I myself
am sick with the finish
put on things

But you're too busy,
too busy for romance;
after all,
a response might tell me,
who you are naked

Who said I should care
What you do
As long as I am free,
You can go fuck yourself:
I don't have to be there

In the Dream

In the dream I was stranded
Amidst the mist and trees
In the dream I was giving someone
A phone number where I
Remained resident but a guest
In the dream you were leaving again
In the dream it was significant
But I did not cry this time
In the dream I had one true
Living relative who'd abandoned me
There were no other friends
In the dream where I had your company
In the dream things grew up around
The grass weaved a knit beneath
Money and kindness only occurred
Where sickness intervened in the dream
In the dream I was not writing this
In the dream I knew was desire and happiness
Music bloomed with easeful care
Character unsuspect, flesh a bliss
In the dream paradise did not leave
A trail against the sunset, below the rail
In the dream I sailed with grace
I did not know there was a place

What You Need

Suicide is not an act, but
A series
Of events, degrees
Retreats and defeats
Brought back
To engorge the throat and sense
S of anything and everything
To culminate and
Slide down
With a leaning
Until
 There is one thing
That they do not
Say, and you won't hear
Defines you, without
Opposition
Where you decide and finally agree.

Convulsion
for John Baker

No one ever moved like this:
stiff with history, still
into strange perfection.
The highways crossed, the moment
gone. Sick, you did not hear

The thundering machine converge,
to shatter flesh – fix photographs.
All things we touch are loosed:
in those good lies of the sun,
amid the vaults of slow horror.

Haunted Rooms

Gather me in your hands, my love
like a swollen bird, or white-winged
dove, swept upward by the cooling breezes
yet you remain, a city mother with a child formed
by rage, while we are strangers pretending
tenderness who commit this suicide

Those also mad and lonely know and
I suspect you refuse both, unaware of
either your infirmities or the way I bleed
making of us each an unheeding heretic
for what may be
most desired and despised in these entireties

Not That I Am

Not that I am
but I was,
thinking about you

Who came back
blue, with cold:
from the mountains

No passages
uncrossed, no music:
untold now anyhow

Sharbot Lake

Cancer and its casual curse
Remains unspoken, for better
Or worse the winter morning we sweep
Around the curve of Highway 37

Out of the woods and covered trees
The cracking ice, the brittle breeze
Parked deep from the White Lake
Hatchery, the fish frozen cameos

Up the hill to the native restaurant
We'll take bacon and eggs and toast
To satisfy our search for tomorrow
Our Ulyssean voyage for more

Across the drive to The Rising Bun
Bread baked, muffins tossed, all awake
On tombstone highways
Into the town of the Lake, at the top

Of the dawning Cortez hill, the dream
Of trees and blue, the quilt of scenes
From another life we borrow now
As it fills the cup of steam arising from the snow

Spies

You can tell me what to no other you'd confess
the secret desires for revenge the depthless measure
of your enmity against the world the many regrets

The idea you or I would confess and speak
what won't be said in this sacrifice
exactly why we meet like this

Lovers of some destiny which claims
what deed and thought cannot control
won't be taught by enemies eavesdropping now

Fifth Column

Your mental patient
your frightened child
Your valiant labor
your devotion to disguise
Your operation of hatred
your fuel for disease
Your criminal deceit
your crippled insanity
Your honored society of mothers
and the mediocre

Your orphan's defeat
the man who retreats
Your sister and brother
no other no other
Your gift of self-pity
your splendid unclean no joy no joy
O vanity the brainwashed
Your obscene Mr.Mitty
your whipping boy
The compromise in this melody

Suburban Wilderness

Your permanently unemployable
poet wanders
in his twilight world; totally
broke, bereft of cash,
companionship and equally idle
friends: with
no honest idea of love or romance,
to comfort his loneliness
and hunger, or whatever this most resembles

Now he allows you to eavesdrop
on these secrets,
which will not be kept; too much
longer than we expect,
beyond redemption or some respect
for all this useless labor:
that shows no remorse nor sweat, yet
scars where he is held
trackless now in a suburban wilderness

On Your Wall

Cut along the dotted line of
Ravens and crows, bestride
The fields littered with an oasis
Of small working animals, the
Miniature horses and burros
The statuary of deer and signposts

Remind this is the world, before
The snow drifts in, a million
Whispers of hey we're here, why
Not disappear, swim across
These roads the pond so still - find
This is not art upon your wall

CPSIA information can be obtained at www.ICGtesting.com
Printed in the USA
LVOW08s1817230315

431675LV00034B/2093/P